Original title:
Dancing Through Life Together

Copyright © 2025 Creative Arts Management OÜ
All rights reserved.

Author: Maxwell Donovan
ISBN HARDBACK: 978-3-69081-268-9
ISBN PAPERBACK: 978-3-69081-764-6

Swaying Under the Starlit Sky

Under the glow of the moon above,
We twirl like figures in a painted glove.
With each misstep, we bump and collide,
But laughter follows us, our joyful guide.

The stars are winking, a cosmic show,
As we trip on toes, moving to and fro.
Our shadows stretch in a silly parade,
While we wobble and giggle, unafraid.

Echoes of Laughter in Our Walk

Side by side, we take silly strides,
With playful nudges and exaggerated glides.
Each step's a joke, a whimsical sway,
And chuckles erupt, come what may.

Footprints in sand, we leave our mark,
With every stumble, we spark a new lark.
As we race the breeze, our spirits take flight,
In this merry chase, everything feels right.

Graceful Turns in the Dance of Life

In a whirl of frolic, around we spin,
With arms wide open, let the fun begin.
We butcher the moves, a comical scene,
Yet every wrong turn reignites the sheen.

Like clumsy puppets, we glide and sway,
With laughter as music, come what may.
With spins that rival a cyclone's twirl,
We embrace the chaos, give it a whirl.

Embracing Each Moment's Beat

Heartbeat kicks, a rhythm so odd,
As we hop like kangaroos, it feels so flawed.
Yet in each blunder, joy finds its place,
With smiles so wide, we own the space.

As time ticks on, we play, we groove,
In this crazy world, we find our move.
With each silly twist, we're never apart,
Crafting memories that speak to the heart.

The Rhythm of Our Souls

We both have two left feet, it's true,
But we step on each other, not the shoe.
In a whirl of giggles, we spin around,
Creating chaos, a joy profound.

With our arms in the air, like we own the floor,
We bump and we stumble, who could ask for more?
Feet in a tangle, we just can't stop,
Our hearts laugh loud, we're the cream of the crop.

Choreography of Companionable Hearts

Like a pair of clumsy penguins on ice,
We slide and we shuffle, not so precise.
Our own little stage, where we take the lead,
In this quirky ballet, we're planting a seed.

With a twirl and a giggle, we stumble some more,
Your laugh makes me trip, oh, what a score!
Grace? It's a myth, but who really cares?
In the mess of our moves, there's magic that spares.

Hand in Hand Through Twists and Turns

We twist and we turn, like a rollercoaster ride,
With you by my side, I take it in stride.
The world spins around us in vibrant hues,
Every wrong step brings us more to lose.

Yet through all the fumbles, the laughter erupts,
Like juggling jellybeans, we're hopelessly cupped.
In this silly tango, we find joy that shines,
Our partnership blooms, defying the lines.

Harmonies of Two

Like a cat on a keyboard, we make quite a sound,
With our offbeat rhythm, we spin round and round.
Silly serenades float through the air,
As our melodies clash, we twirl with flair.

We compose a duet in a quirky, mad dash,
With every misstep leading to a splash.
In the symphony of life, so wobbly and sweet,
Together, my dear, we make it complete.

Whirlwinds of Togetherness

In a kitchen we twirl, bumping the fridge,
Spinning like tops, with a roll and a smidge.
Flour is flying, oh what a sight,
Laughter erupts, such pure delight.

The vacuum calls, we slide on the floor,
Pretending to glide, with a dramatic roar.
The room is our stage, where we laugh and we tease,
Chasing our shadows, moving with ease.

We trip over pillows, we twirl 'round the chair,
Each moment a dance that brings joy to the air.
Falling in laughter, we land with a thump,
Together we rise from each humorous lump.

In life's little whirlwinds, we find our own way,
With giggles and grins, come what may.
Each silly routine, a unforgettable ride,
Hand in hand, we're the jesters with pride.

Journeys in Perfect Time

With mismatched socks, we hit the road,
Shopping for snacks, laughter bestowed.
In the car we bop, to our favorite tune,
Shaking our heads, no one else in the room.

We dance at red lights, just you and me,
Invading the world with our wild jubilee.
Each honk is a trumpet, our feet tap away,
To the rhythm of joy, come join in our play.

We stumble on sidewalk, with snacks in our hands,
The giggles erupt, our own little bands.
Sharing our stories, oh what a delight,
Creating memories that sparkle so bright.

Life is a journey, one step at a time,
With laughter and love, everything's prime.
In every wrong turn, a new dance begins,
With you by my side, oh the joy that it brings!

Spirited Motion in Quiet Moments

In the quiet of mornings, a warm cup in hand,
We swirl like two leaves in a whimsical band.
The bacon sizzles, we twirl in our seats,
Our joyfully dulcet, two playful beats.

As laundry spins 'round, we take on the chore,
Fighting for space on the floor by the door.
Wiggling and jostling, folding in time,
To our own chorus, everything's prime.

With silly routines, the dishes all stack,
We swirl like two magnets, no looking back.
A playful pat here, a twirl with a grin,
Life's little moments, where laughter begins.

In each quiet instant, our hearts intertwine,
Joyful foxtrots of life, where our spirits align.
Together we gather, in whispers we play,
In a world full of laughter, we brightened the day.

A Celebration of Togetherness

On this funny path, we take little leaps,
With faces that crinkle, and laughter that keeps.
A tickle, a nudge, it's the game that we play,
In the festival of us, come join the ballet.

Under the moonlight, we trip down the lane,
With echoes of giggles, in sunshine or rain.
Sideways glances, a skip to the beat,
Two partners in silliness, happy and sweet.

The cake is a mess, what a comical sight,
Faces covered with frosting, oh what a delight!
Each bite that we share, is a reason to cheer,
For every little joy, when together, my dear.

So let's raise a glass to our whimsical dance,
With sparks in our eyes, we'll sing and prance.
In this jubilant world, may the laughter resound,
For the joy of togetherness is truly profound.

Unwritten Choreography of Us

In mismatched socks we twirl and sway,
With bunny hops and silly plays,
You step on toes, I laugh out loud,
Our goofy moves could please a crowd.

The cat joins in, quite unimpressed,
She rolls her eyes, we're just obsessed,
With every spin and jolly jig,
We're a strange duo, oh so big!

A zesty dip, a playful tease,
Your tickle fight brings me to my knees,
Through every mishap and little slip,
Our rhythm grows, we're on this trip.

With no grand rules, we make it free,
This quirky dance of you and me,
So when we falter, just hold on tight,
We'll laugh it off, we'll make it right.

Together We Spin the World

We whirl like leaves on autumn's breeze,
Inventing moves with utmost ease,
You lead with flair, I join the ride,
Our laughter echoes far and wide.

Your wild spins cause a smudge or two,
I trip and giggle, what a view!
With every twirl, we paint the sky,
Two clumsy stars, oh me, oh my!

A waddle here, a shimmy there,
We leap and bound without a care,
With flailing arms and silly grins,
This is where our fun begins.

The coffee pot joins, it starts to jig,
The toast pops up, it's quite the gig,
With pancake flips and syrup drips,
Together we laugh, through all the flips.

Synchronized Beyond Words

You grab the broom, I seize the mop,
We're cleaning up with a little hop,
As dust bunnies twirl, they start to fly,
Our kitchen concert, oh my, oh my!

With every sweep, we make a beat,
In this wild mess, we find our feet,
The fridge starts humming a catchy tune,
We shimmy past the old vacuumed croon.

In perfect sync, we toss the trash,
A glittering scene, with a golden flash,
As socks get tossed and spaghetti spins,
In our world of chaos, the laughter wins!

So here we dance, with joy and cheer,
Creating smiles, year after year,
With every step, our hearts entwine,
In this funny dance, we truly shine.

The Tango of Our Days

We hop like frogs through morning's light,
Your coffee spills with a giggly fright,
The dog barks loud, he thinks it's play,
As you tease and twirl throughout the day.

At noon we lunch with sandwiches wide,
We toast with juice as we slide and glide,
Your funny faces make me grin,
This silly life, let's take a spin!

The laundry spins while we do a jig,
With socks and shirts, it's quite a gig,
We fold with flair, each wrinkle's a chance,
To polish our moves with a silly dance.

As stars come out and the day unwinds,
We burst with laughter, no one mind,
With every twirl, our hearts align,
In this crazy tango, you are mine.

Twirls in Unison

In mismatched shoes we prance around,
With silly twirls, we lose our ground.
You step on toes, I laugh out loud,
In this wild dance, we're far from proud.

The cat looks on, all eyes ablaze,
As we fumble through our clumsy phase.
Your ankle's caught, a table's there!
We tumble down without a care.

With giggles high and arms all wide,
We twirl in sync, each other's guide.
Forget the beat, let's make our own,
In this grand ball, we've fully grown.

So here's to us, the comical pair,
Two left feet, but we hardly care.
With goofy grins and laughter sweet,
Our love's a dance, so funny and neat.

Together We Spin

We whirl and spin through snack-filled nights,
With pizza slices, our greatest delights.
You drop your drink; it spills, oh gee!
Yet still, we dance with wild glee.

A twirl here, a spin there, watch me trip,
Climbing over each other with every flip.
The dog's joined in, chasing our feet,
In this silly toss, no chance to retreat.

Our moves are wild, like grasshoppers' play,
Each twist a laugh, stealing the day.
With wink and nod, and a silly jig,
We've choreographed our mischief big.

So let's keep spinning 'til we're dizzy,
With ice cream cones, and moments busy.
In this wacky waltz, we truly blend,
Two clowns in rhythm, no need to pretend.

Choreography of Souls

Our steps resemble a tangled yarn,
With each new move, we raise alarm.
You shout a beat, and I respond,
With flailing arms and legs far beyond.

The mirror reflects our comical sight,
As we scramble left, then dash to the right.
I trip on a mat, you giggle with glee,
Between fits of laughter, we just might flee.

We may not shine like the stars above,
But with our quirks, we dance with love.
In every shuffle, a heartfelt cheer,
Our souls are twirling, drawing near.

So here's to our dance, a chaotic blend,
In every stumble, we find a friend.
With giggles echoing, our spirits soar,
This wacky shuffle is what we adore.

Whirling in Harmony

In mismatched socks, we start our show,
You lead the way as I follow slow.
With each wrong step, we bust a move,
Laughing so hard, we start to groove.

The cat on the shelf gives us a stare,
As we pirouette without a care.
You try the splits, end up on the floor,
Yet burst out laughing, craving more.

We twine around like spaghetti art,
Creating laughter in every part.
With whirls and bumps, our joy ignites,
In this silly saunter, we reach new heights.

So let's keep whirling, round and round,
In this ballet of joy, our love's profound.
With every twist and turn, we flee,
Two hearts in sync, forever free.

Movements of Love and Laughter

We twirl like socks in a dryer spin,
Spinning so fast, let the giggles begin.
With moves so silly, we conquer the floor,
Who knew clumsiness could open a door?

Our feet sometimes tangle, a comedic show,
Like two lost kittens, we put on a glow.
You step on my toes, then I'll step on yours,
Together we laugh, forget all the chores.

Sometimes we trip, and that's part of the game,
Each fall brings a chuckle, a silly new name.
With every misstep, our hearts seem to soar,
Life's just a dance, so let's ask for more!

So let's dance in pajamas, in sunshine or rain,
Life's a wild party, come join the fun train.
With love in our steps, and laughter on cue,
Two joyful hearts waltzing, just me and you.

Cadence of Dreams Unfolding

We leap like frogs on a bright sunny day,
Each hop brings a giggle, come join in the play.
Our wobbly rhythms make everyone cheer,
In this silly jig, we've nothing to fear.

With pirouettes that spin like a top,
We find our own groove and never quite stop.
Your arm is my guide, your laugh is the beat,
Together we shuffle, feel light on our feet.

Laughter's the loop that keeps us in sync,
We gesture and mime, raise our glasses and clink.
Our hearts create music, our souls start to sing,
In this choreography, love's the grand fling.

With dreams in our pockets, in each other we trust,
Life's a comic ballet, not just a must.
So let's waddle and wander wherever we roam,
Each quirky step leads us closer to home.

Partners in Every Turn

In the spotlight's glow, we spin and we sway,
Each turn is a tickle, don't want it to stray.
With giggles and snorts, we glide through the air,
Two peas in a pod, what a wobbly pair!

When we trip over nothing, oh what a sight,
We laugh 'til we cry, it brings pure delight.
You lead with a grin, I follow with glee,
In this dance of mishaps, we're wild and free.

Our feet work in concert, like well-tuned guitars,
With choruses of chuckles, under the stars.
We waddle and stumble, make up our own rules,
In this rhythmic chaos, we're nobody's fools.

The music's our laughter, the stars are our guide,
Together we twist, with arms open wide.
Here's to all the blunders that make our hearts yearn,
With each silly moment, together we learn.

The Glow of Shared Steps

With shadows a-dancing beneath the moonlight,
We jiggle and wobble, it feels just right.
Every stumble a treasure, each giggle a sound,
In the rhythm of friendship, true joy can be found.

Our toes elegantly clash, like popcorn in a pot,
Each bounce sends a ripple, we're trouble not caught.
With your goofy grin, and my oh-so-smooth spin,
In this whimsical waltz, we always win.

We shuffle and sway, in mismatched old shoes,
Our hearts sing in harmony, wearing love's hues.
With every strange step, we weave tales anew,
In a dance of delight, it's just me and you.

So here's to our journey, wherever it goes,
In this joyful ballet, the laughter just flows.
Together we'll twirl, a vibrant display,
With hearts intertwined, we'll dance every day.

Sundrenched Twirls in the Afternoon

We spin like tops in summer's blaze,
Our shadows stretch in playful ways.
With every laugh, our bodies sway,
Who knew a stroll could feel like play?

In flip-flops flying, we trip and laugh,
Chasing the breeze like a silly calf.
With each silly step, we make a scene,
What fun we find in the space between!

Wobbly knees, who needs a beat?
We choreograph our dorky feet.
With the sun as our sparkling guide,
We flail and giggle with nothing to hide.

Stumbling close, a dance-floor fail,
We laugh so hard, it never pales.
In this sunny, silly grace,
Let's twirl until we lose our place.

Crescendo of Connection

With goofy moves, we join the beat,
Our laughter spills like candy sweet.
A clumsy turn, a twinkling smile,
We ripple through the crowd, a funny style.

Clapping hands and wiggly hips,
In our own world, we flip and skip.
A misstep here, a snorty cheer,
Together our joy beats loud and clear.

We twirl and dip, then bump the wall,
A wind-up toy, we can't stand tall.
With every beat, we twist and shout,
And who cares if we fall about?

Our silly flair brings smiles anew,
A symphony of oddity, just us two.
In this waltz of giggles, we unite,
A crescendo made of pure delight.

Pirouetting Under the Moonlight

Beneath the stars, we spin around,
In our own world, we've lost all sound.
A shoe goes flying, off it sails,
We laugh till we cry, we'll tell the tales.

With twirls so grand, we grip the night,
A comedy show, oh what a sight!
The moon beams down, an audience rare,
As we create our own midnight air.

A quick misstep sends us both down,
Rolling along, not a worry, no frown.
Giggling softly, we rise again,
With comic grace, we both pretend.

Together in this moonlit spree,
Light as feathers, wild and free.
In laughter's rhythm, we find our tune,
Oh, what a night beneath the moon!

Motion in the Space Between Us

Each little jiggle, a silly dance,
In our own bubble, we take a chance.
In crowded places, we spin like larks,
Drawing smiles as we spark our marks.

With shimmies and shakes, we steal the show,
An impromptu ballet, don't you know?
Fumbling gestures, yet hearts are bright,
In the space between, we share delight.

Our feet get tangled, yet we don't stop,
Two goofy souls, on top we hop.
We make our own rules, bumping and swerving,
In every chuckle, love is enduring.

So here's to rhythms that we create,
Through clumsy moves, oh, isn't it great?
In our whirlwind of joy, we find our place,
Just two oddballs, embracing the space.

Treading Softly in Unison

We tiptoe on the kitchen floor,
Like spies in a comic dance-off lore.
The dog joins in, tail-wagging joy,
As we twirl, oh what a noise!

With mismatched socks and goofy grins,
We stomp like elephants, laughter spins.
The cat gives us a judging stare,
While we pirouette, floating in air.

Gliding past the laundry pile,
With each move, we provoke a smile.
A tumble, a roll, we both collide,
In this silly game, we just can't hide.

With every step, we find our groove,
In this vibrant mess, our feet will move.
Together we spin, a playful sight,
As the world fades, and our hearts take flight.

Spirals of Togetherness

In the living room, we make a mess,
With twirling bodies and playful excess.
A coffee cup soars, nearly a hit,
As we spin around, full of wit.

The vacuum cleaner starts to hum,
And suddenly, we both become numb.
We dance with the dust bunnies in the air,
Giggling softly, without a care.

With hands up high, we start the chase,
Around the couch, we quicken our pace.
Each corner we round, it's a laugh anew,
Mimicking birds—then the cat joins too!

As music blares from the old radio,
We bust out moves like a freak show.
With each twist and turn, we break the mold,
Our spiral of joy is pure gold.

The Waltz of Our Shared Stories

Once upon a time, we both did sway,
In the kitchen, lost in a butter play.
With spatulas raised and an apron dance,
Every mishap led to a wild romance.

The stories blend like a bright paintbrush,
Each moment shared, we find a rush.
Skipping past spills and little regrets,
We laugh at ourselves, no need for resets.

In the tale of socks that vanished one day,
We twirled to the rhythm of disarray.
Every mishap, a chapter, a verse,
In this funny world, we couldn't be worse.

As the clock ticks, we sway on cue,
With memories rich, we dance anew.
A waltz of chaos, a storybook plot,
Two goofy souls in a whimsical knot.

Footprints in the Sand of Time

On a sunny beach, we start to stride,
With every step, we turn the tide.
Footprints scattered, a comical sight,
As we chase the waves with pure delight.

In the sand, we write our names,
Silly doodles and prancing games.
A seagull swoops down, eyes on our snack,
While we laugh and giggle—oh, what a quack!

With buckets and shovels, we dig a moat,
Building a kingdom, but oh, what a bloat.
A spectacular castle that crumbles so fast,
Leaving us in giggles, whatever the past.

As the sun dips low with a golden hue,
We dance on the beach, just me and you.
With each wave that crashes, we laugh and glide,
In the footprints of time, we take this ride.

Verses of the Heart's Cadence.

With each twirl, we trip and spin,
Our feet collide; let the fun begin!
In mismatched socks and joyful glee,
We laugh so hard, it's plain to see.

You step on my toes, I say, "Oh dear!"
You giggle back, 'It's part of the cheer!'
With every stumble, we find a way,
To dance like nobody's watching today.

Our rhythm's a joke, a slapstick tease,
We leap and glide like leaves in the breeze.
Each spin brings new twists, and giggles rise,
Together we shimmer, under bright skies.

So here's to our steps, though clumsy and wild,
We partner through life, forever beguiled.
With every hiccup, a new laugh springs,
As we waltz through the chaos that each moment brings.

Waltzing on the Edge of Dreams

We sway on the brink of a marshmallow pie,
Two jellybeans bouncing, oh me, oh my!
Our shoes are too big, but that's quite alright,
We'll leap like two frogs in the soft twilight.

A tango with chaos, a jig with the moon,
Our laughter's a melody that plays every noon.
With each silly spin, and each playful glance,
We waltz through our dreams in a gooey romance.

Hippos in tutus on a dance floor of cheer,
Sometimes we wobble, but never shed a tear.
Just twirling along, making friends with the fun,
Two bubbly hearts shining bright like the sun.

As starlight invites us to join in the spree,
We'll take silly bows, just you wait and see!
With hearts in a whirl, we embrace every scheme,
For life's just a stage, and we're living the dream!

Two Hearts in Syncopated Motion

In a room full of slippers, we sneak to the floor,
Flopping like fish, holding onto the door.
With giggles erupting at each little slip,
We're planning our moves like a carnival trip.

You lead the cha-cha, my two left feet,
I'm hopping and skipping, what a wild feat!
With popcorn and props, our dance is a show,
We spin and we bounce, just go with the flow.

A shuffle, a wiggle, with spaghetti arms,
We juggle our laughter, avoiding all harms.
With silly old hats perched high on our heads,
We throw caution out, let the caution fly—treads!

So here on the floor, in our goofy parade,
We'll make silly memories, no need to be staid.
With each quirky step, we'll burst into song,
Two hearts in bright motion, where we both belong.

A Journey in Step

We march along paths with our shoes so mismatched,
Tripping on dreams, but oh, how we've snatched!
With a hop and a skip, we explore the strange roads,
While dodging the puddles and extra-large toads.

A barnyard boogie, with cows joining in,
Our feet keep on tapping, like it's a sin!
With laughter in waves, we glide through the muck,
Chasing down rainbows, just a bit of good luck.

In rhythm we ramble, with giggles and whirls,
Our adventures as bright as a bubble of pearls.
On this silly journey, through giggles and cheer,
We conquer the world, one laugh at a year!

So hand in hand, let's hop through the day,
In a field full of sunflowers, we'll dance and sway.
With joy overflowing, we'll never lose sight,
Of the strange little steps that make life feel right.

Steps in Perfect Harmony

Two left feet on the floor, it's true,
We trip and laugh, me and you.
A salsa of giggles, a waltz of clums,
As we twirl through life, our joy hums.

With mismatched socks and shoes that squeak,
We rumble and tumble, both unique.
You step on toes, I take a fall,
Yet, in this chaos, we have it all.

Two hearts in sync, though rhythm's a mess,
We shimmy through each little stress.
In silly hats, we prance around,
Our laugh track plays, a joyful sound.

So, let's twirl to our own beat,
In this lovely dance, life is sweet.
For every slip, a new surprise,
Together we shine, no need for disguise.

A Duet Across the Days

We start the morning with coffee and spins,
Your goofy grin is where it begins.
With spoons as microphones, we belt out tunes,
Our kitchen concerts in pajama costumes.

A shuffle to work, but I can't keep pace,
You break into laughter, oh my, what a race!
With lunch breaks spent in silly rhymes,
We groove through deadlines, our perfect crimes.

The evening sun paints shadows that sway,
While you juggle dinner in a playful display.
Each failed attempt brings chuckles galore,
Our gourmet chaos, who could want more?

So here's to the days of playful delight,
With you by my side, everything's right.
A duet of laughter, a song we adore,
As we dance through the years and create evermore.

Pirouettes on the Path of Time

Round and round, we spin with glee,
Time's a whimsy, just you and me.
In mismatched shoes, we leap and bound,
Our own little show where joy is found.

Your twirls send my heart in a spin,
A backward shuffle, but still we win.
With giggly grins and inelegant flair,
We tumble in sync, unaware of the glare.

From dawn's first light to the twilight's sigh,
We take silly bets on who will fly.
Each pirouette tells a funny tale,
In this crazy ballet, we will prevail.

So let's leap through life, a comical dance,
With pratfalls and laughter, we take our chance.
For every misstep, a moment divine,
Together we soar, delightfully entwined.

Whispers of Joy in Every Step

As we shuffle through puddles on a rainy day,
You splash and you giggle, what more can I say?
With each little leap, a chorus we sing,
Our rhythm of joy is a marvelous thing.

In the midst of the mundane, we find our groove,
With tiny misfires, our feet always move.
You pirouette past, a sight to behold,
Laughter erupts, a treasure untold.

The sidewalks become our playful stage,
With imaginations that never age.
We shimmy and shake, a beautiful mess,
Together we frolic, life's quirky address.

So let's stroll through the seasons, hearts light as air,
In whispers of joy, let's dance without care.
For every step, my dear, you're the best part,
With laughter and love, you dance in my heart.

The Ballet of Our Bond

In tutus spun like whirling dervishes,
We trip on toes and send out splinters.
With pirouettes that turn into tumbles,
We laugh it off, no time for grumbles.

Our arms entwined, we leap and flop,
Being graceful, oh, that's a swap!
Ballet slippers with mismatched laces,
In our very own clumsy places.

With every turn, we share a grin,
Who knew we'd twirl and laugh like kin?
The stage is set in our living room,
Where every mistake adds to the bloom.

So here's to us, the clumsy pair,
With laughter and love, we're rare as air.
Between the falls and slapstick flair,
Our bond's a ballet that we both share.

United in Every Step

With two left feet and a heart so bold,
We stomp the ground, like stories told.
In unison we skip, a wild parade,
Side by side, our plans never fade.

We shuffle through life on a wobbly line,
Stolen ice cream and sips of wine.
Step on my toes, I'll push you back,
Together we groove, and that's a fact.

In zigzags and loops, our journey fun,
From sunrise dashes to setting sun.
We'll kick and twirl, not a single care,
With every faux pas, laughter fills the air.

So grab my hand, let's twirl around,
With giggles and grins, we're never bound.
In our goofy waltz, we're a silly tribe,
United forever, can't let it slide!

Chasing Dreams with Open Hearts

With wild hearts and mismatched socks,
We chase the dreams like feathered flocks.
In a whirlwind of whimsy, we run and race,
With jubilant giggles and silly face.

Through puddles we leap, splashing away,
Turning the mundane into a play.
With every stumble, joy becomes clear,
The world's our dance floor, let's draw near.

As we map out a life with hilarious blunders,
We write our story while smiling like thunder.
Collecting the moments that tickle our souls,
In his lopsided cap and my rainbow shoals.

So let's cast worries into the blue,
And chase after dreams with a goofy crew.
Holding hands tight, we'll never part,
In the goofy dance of a foolish heart.

Together We Write Our Song

With a swing and a sway, we start our tune,
Two serenaders beneath a bright moon.
Our rhythm's a riddle, a silly affair,
With every missed note, we just don't care.

The lyrics are scribbled, just playful from start,
With verses of laughter that echo heart to heart.
In harmonies tangled and giggly refrains,
We waltz through the chaos, forget all the pains.

Our jingle's a blast on the streets we roam,
Making grand noise as we sing from home.
With spoons as our instruments, pots as our drums,
Together we're silly—a troupe of love's sums.

So here's to our song, off-beat but sweet,
A melody messy, but makes us complete.
With smiles on our faces, we'll sing all day long,
In the chorus of life, we happily belong.

Embrace the Pulse of Togetherness

Twirl in socks on kitchen floors,
Spin around as the cat explores.
With every step, the laughter flies,
Who knew two left feet could win the prize?

Grocery aisles become our stage,
With cart ballet, we engage.
The neighbor's dog joins the fun,
Our little show has just begun!

Each goofy move, a grin we share,
We trip, we stumble, but we don't care.
Wobbling through this waltz of ours,
Finding joy beneath the stars!

In silly hats, we do confess,
Our awkward rhythms are the best.
So let's embrace this quirky dance,
In each misstep, we find romance!

The Soft Stomp of Shared Adventures

With raucous laughs we hit the road,
A mismatched pair, our antics flowed.
The radio sings our favorite tunes,
While we stomp our feet like wild raccoons!

Sipping coffee, hiccupping loud,
Not a chance to blend with the crowd.
In every stop, we find a joke,
Life's a sketch, and we're the poke!

Picnic tables rock and sway,
Who knew a sandwich could play?
As crumbs become our shaky fate,
We laugh like children—ain't it great?

Our clumsy steps lead the way,
Into the night, where shadows play.
In this circus act of ours,
The soft stomp brings us all the pow'rs!

Heartbeats in Melody

Every heartbeat a comical song,
We sway and sway, can't go wrong.
With silly grins and wobbly knees,
Our quirky duet puts life at ease.

The metronome ticks in triple-time,
We shimmy along, oh so sublime.
Our rhythm might be out of tune,
Yet joy drops in like a big balloon!

In the kitchen, we draft our plans,
With spatulas as magic wands.
And every clap's a syncopate,
Pasta raves on our dinner plate!

Swaying to every silly beat,
Heartbeats dance, and we repeat.
In joyful chaos, we find our way,
Every moment's a fun ballet!

The Flow of Our Journey

Life's a river, so let's float,
With rapids wild, and funny quotes.
A paddle in hand, we splash and grin,
This whimsical ride, oh where to begin?

Raccoons applaud with claps so loud,
As we tip, tumble, but feel so proud.
Over waterfalls, we take a dive,
Giggling madly, oh how we thrive!

In this boat, we sing our song,
Tunes of mishaps, where we belong.
The journey's full of twists and bends,
Every curve with laughter blends!

So hold on tight, let's glide and swerve,
With every ripple, we've got the nerve.
This flowing tale brings joy anew,
In every splash, it's me and you!

Waltzing in the Moonlight

Underneath the glowing beams,
We spin like two silly schemes.
With each misstep, laughter blooms,
As shadows jiggle in our rooms.

A twirl, a trip, a giggled shout,
We float around; there's no doubt.
Our feet may fumble, but oh what fun,
Two stars colliding, we can't be outdone!

Sway of Hearts

In the kitchen, we sway and glide,
With spatulas and pots as our guide.
We shimmy past the fridge and stove,
Creating a whirl of our own little grove.

With a dip and a dash, the flour flies,
As we dance with chaos in our eyes.
The cake may burn, but who really cares?
We waltz through the smoke, and laughter declares!

Steps in Time

One step forward, then two back,
Our rhythm's off, it's a fun attack.
We laugh at our steps, oh what a sight,
Like two clumsy goats in a moonlit night.

On the sidewalk, we prance and sway,
Stumbling as if we've lost our way.
But with each giggle, we play our part,
In the great ballet of the silly heart.

Rhythm of Our Journey

We shuffle our feet on a bumpy road,
Every bump adds to the goofy load.
With each little jig, our troubles fade,
As we laugh at the puns that we both made.

Through puddles and mud, our dance unfolds,
Each hop and skip, a story told.
In this merry jig, with grins so wide,
We dance through the mess, side by side.

Side by Side in Life's Ballet

We twirl and spin with glee,
Tripping over each other's feet.
In perfect time, we laugh so bright,
Two clowns in a spotlight.

With every leap and awkward turn,
We face plant, then we learn.
Our pirouettes may go astray,
Yet joy is here to stay.

In tutus made of dish cloths,
We perform for our small dogs.
The neighbors peek, a silent cheer,
Imagine the fun we hold dear!

Our stage is set, the crowd's our cat,
A wild audience, imagine that!
We bow with pride, a sight so rare,
Life's ballet, a funny affair.

Our Lives, a Rhythmic Narrative

With every beat, we fumble forth,
Our steps of joy prove their worth.
In sync we glide, a clumsy show,
Waving at crowds, we steal the show.

A misstep here, a laugh beyond,
We sway along, a life so fond.
With goofy grins, we take the lead,
In this rhythmic tale, we both proceed.

Amidst the giggles, a silent cheer,
Our hearts collide, can't help but steer.
Together we leap, no pair is smarter,
Unless we slip on the floor like an otter!

Each laugh echoes in the air,
With silly moves, we simply dare.
Our narrative flows with every prank,
In this dance, there's no room for rank.

From Stars to Sidewalks, We Move

In starlit nights, we often glide,
Over cracks, we take our stride.
With each misstep, a giggly squeal,
We face the world with zest and zeal.

Our journey's paved with quirky grace,
With funny hats, we own the place.
Underneath the moon's soft glance,
We trip and laugh, join the dance.

From sidewalks cracked to cosmic heights,
Our hearts align with joyful flights.
With every fall, we rise anew,
In cosmic chaos, me and you.

As starlight dances in our view,
We step in sync, just us two.
Hold tight to fun, let worries flee,
In a wobbly world, you're my glee.

Embracing Every Beat

Let's embrace the clumsiness with flair,
As we hop and skip without a care.
A funky beat takes us away,
In our own silly world, we sway.

With hands in the air and feet in a mess,
In every twirl, we find success.
Our laughter echoes, a joyful part,
As we groove along, heart to heart.

We shake and wobble, oh what a sight!
Two goofballs sharing delight.
Our dance is more than steps; it's a game,
And laughably odd, it's all the same.

So let's sway to life, both near and far,
As we glide by, just like a star.
In each little beat, we find our song,
In this wild ride, we both belong.

The Dance of Resilience

In mismatched socks, we whirl and sway,
Tripping on toes in a comical play.
With laughter as our guiding beat,
We spin through the chaos, never admit defeat.

Life's clumsy steps may cause us to fall,
Yet we rise up, having a ball.
Our rhythm may falter, but hearts stay bold,
In this goofy waltz, our stories unfold.

From the tumble of heels to the slide of shoes,
We embrace each misstep, it's ours to choose.
With chuckles our anthem, we shimmy and glide,
In this grand performance, joy is our guide.

So here's to the stumbles as life takes a twirl,
With a smile on our faces, let's give it a whirl!
Together we tango through thick and through thin,
In the dance of resilience, we both always win.

Flowing with the Current

Like ducks in a pond, we paddled along,
Making ripples of laughter, our silly song.
With our feet in the water and love in our sails,
We swim through the days, telling goofy tales.

A boat full of dreams, we sail in a twist,
Navigating life's waters, none can resist.
With splashes and giggles, we float side by side,
In this wild journey, we learn how to ride.

The current may surge, and the wind might howl,
But we navigate storms with a wink and a growl.
Through waves of absurdity, each stroke we embrace,
With joy in our hearts, we dance with grace.

So let's drift through the whirl, let not the grin fade,
With humor our anchor, we'll never evade.
In the river of life, may our laughter resound,
As we flow through the current, with joy all around.

Hearts in Syncopation

With feet that stumble and flail about,
We whirl in circles, there's no room for doubt.
Our hearts beat a rhythm that's unique and free,
In this cacophony, pure harmony we see.

Two jigsaw puzzles with pieces amiss,
A clunky duet, but what a sweet bliss!
With a chuckle and grin, we laugh off the flaws,
In our goofy ballet, we create our own laws.

From the tiny missteps to the grand pirouette,
We embrace the strange tunes that life has met.
In a duet of folly, we tango through jest,
With goofy precision, we're truly the best.

Hearts beat in sync when we spin round and round,
In this comic caper, true magic is found.
As larks in the spotlight, we dance with delight,
Together we waltz through the wildest of nights.

Lyrical Journeys

With every step, a chuckle escapes,
Our journey's a sitcom, full of funny shapes.
On this lyrical path, we sway with the breeze,
In our whimsical world, we dance with such ease.

From karaoke nights to hopscotch disgrace,
We leap through life, setting our own pace.
In the rhythm of nonsense, our spirits take flight,
With joy as our compass, everything feels right.

In a conga line formed by sheer accident,
We twirl and we giggle, love's our frequent event.
Through stumbling and fumbling, we find our own song,
With each quirky note, we'll always belong.

So here's to the jigs that we come to create,
In this lyrical journey, we celebrate fate.
As we wander our path with laughter and cheer,
Together we dance, year after year.

The Dance of Mutual Dreams

In socks that slip on wooden floors,
We spin and twirl, a laugh restores.
With pizza crumbs upon our clothes,
We're modern dancers, as everyone knows.

In dinner chairs, we rock and sway,
Our rhythms clash, yet lead the way.
With every stumble, chuckles burst,
Life's waltz is fun, and never cursed.

The cat looks on, bemused and sweet,
As we perform our silly feat.
With every step, our hearts entwine,
Each moment shared, a mountain climbed.

So let the music lift us high,
We'll leap and bound; give it a try!
In this wild embrace, we elevate,
Two hearts in rhythm, we celebrate.

Interwoven Paths of Joy

Two left feet find their way to dance,
In mismatched shoes, we take a chance.
Step on one's toes, then laugh it off,
Life's a party, so let's scoff.

In kitchens bright with bowls and flour,
We sway like trees, each one a tower.
Baking cookies, then chasing crumbs,
Our laughter echoes, drumming thuds.

Through clumsy jigs and pirouettes,
We twirl around without regrets.
When giggles spark, the fun ignites,
Our shared frolics reach new heights.

With every slip, a memory made,
In fleeting rhythms, we parlayed.
Life's grand ballet unfolds its charm,
Together we move, arm in arm.

When Two Souls Meet on the Floor

With two left shoes, you spin me 'round,
We kick and laugh, our joys profound.
The record skips, just like our feet,
In this absurdity, we find bliss sweet.

In the living room, the world disappears,
With every bump, we shed our fears.
Your goofy grin ignites the spark,
Together we dance in daylight or dark.

We invent rhythms, laugh like kids,
Two silly fools who just can't quit.
With each misstep, we cheer and shout,
Life's the party; there's no doubt.

So let's sway wildly, forget the tune,
As joy erupts beneath the moon.
In our vibrant whirl, we find the score,
Two souls alight, forevermore.

Two Bodies, One Symphony

We shuffle and hop, in syncopated glee,
Your laughter echoes, a joyful decree.
With rubbery limbs and awkward flair,
Our quirky jig draws puzzled stares.

In crowded places, we spark a scene,
Two merry misfits; we reign as king and queen.
Tripping over the beat, we toss aside care,
With spins and twirls, we fill the air.

When the music fades, we still hum loud,
A silly duo, we make ourselves proud.
With every shake, we rattle the floor,
Two bodies united, craving more.

Our comic ballet lights up the night,
Sharing giggles and twirls with delight.
In every stumble, love's melody swells,
Together we dance — oh, can't you tell?

Rhapsody of the Everyday

In socks that slide and slippers squeak,
We whirl around, oh what a peek!
Missed the couch while trying to boogie,
Now I'm on the floor, feeling quite zany.

With cereal dances at breakfast hours,
We're champions in our PJs, wielding powers.
Laughs and spills as the mornings blend,
Each clumsy move, a joy we send.

Even chores turn into our merry tune,
Dusting with flair, mocking the moon.
The vacuum's a partner, it hums along,
As we two-step, our hearts sing strong.

Life's stage is set with giggles galore,
Every mishap opens a brand-new door.
In every misstep, we find delight,
Turning our struggles into pure light.

A Love That Twirls

In kitchen corners, we spin like pros,
Flipping pancakes, oh how they pose!
Caught in a twirl, I miss the plate,
Your laughter echoes, isn't this fate?

Our living room's a grand ballet,
With cats as critics, they sass and play.
We leap over toys, dodging the mess,
From tiptoes to tumbles, we are blessed.

On rainy days, we march in sync,
Jumping in puddles, oh how we wink!
Umbrellas flip and then take flight,
Laughter rains down, heart's pure delight.

Every day a dance, a silly new quest,
With outstretched arms, we give our best.
In joyful chaos, our spirits soar,
Together in laughter, forevermore.

Flowing Like a River's Embrace

We wade through streams of daily grind,
With silly splashes, laughter intertwined.
Floating downstream on that old canoe,
Paddles clashing, paint skies blue.

Each grocery run's a grand escape,
With cart races that we joyfully shape.
Dodging the aisles, we go full throttle,
Creating a ruckus, oh what a bottle!

Side by side in quirky attire,
Our hearts ignite, setting the world on fire.
If life's a river, then let's mislead,
Through bends and turns, it's you I need.

In the whirlpools of mundane strife,
We swim in giggles, that's our life.
With every ripple, we cruise and cheer,
Together forever, my dear, my dear.

Celestial Steps Beneath Us

Underneath the stars, we awkwardly prance,
Tripping through cosmos, no time for romance.
With each silly stumble, the moon shakes its head,
Yet we just laugh, not a single shred.

In our makeshift disco, we spin around,
With disco balls made of tinfoil found.
Shadows flicker like stars on the floor,
Giggling so hard, we can't take much more.

Comets are jealous of our wild moves,
As we glide and glide, no need to prove.
Through stardust dreams, our laughter flies,
In this cosmic chaos, our love never lies.

With constellations as our guiding light,
We'll chase the comets through the dark night.
Each twirl a promise, a cosmic jest,
In this universe, we surely are blessed.

Swirling Through the Years

Twirls and spins in mismatched shoes,
Making up steps we sometimes lose.
Laughter echoes, bright and clear,
As we glide through each silly year.

Falling over, we both agree,
Life's a dance, just you and me.
With each stumble, we find our groove,
Together, there's nothing we can't prove.

Flip and flap like a fish in the sea,
Who knew rhythm would set us free?
With giggles puffing like a balloon,
Swaying together beneath the moon.

So let's rhythmically trip down the lane,
Waltz through the fun and embrace the pain.
For every misstep, a chuckle's found,
In our quirky groove, we're tightly bound.

The Waltz of Togetherness

Two left feet in a right-foot world,
With every misstep, our laughter swirled.
A spin, a slide, we take a chance,
Right into a world where we both prance.

You lead, I follow, but wait, I'll steal,
The rhythm of life becomes our wheel.
With silly hats and mismatched attire,
We strut through each day, never tire.

We twirl like penguins in a snowstorm,
Finding our style, embracing the norm.
Every clumsy twirl, a joy to preserve,
In our waltz, it's laughter we serve.

As we groove through puddles and skies,
In our merry jig, we light up the highs.
With every giggle, the world spins bright,
Together we revel, into the night.

Echoes of Laughter

In the hall of giggles, we take our stand,
With foot-tapping beats, oh so unplanned.
We trip and we tumble, oh what a sight,
But in our ruckus, everything feels right.

The clatter of feet, a joyous tune,
As we swirl and whizz 'neath the bright moon.
Every chuckle rings, a melody sweet,
In our silly dance, no one skips a beat.

With each spinning act, a story unfolds,
Of tossing our cares like glittering gold.
And when we collide like balloons in the air,
We giggle and waddle without a care.

So here's to the joy in the chaos we bring,
With laughter as music, our hearts warmly sing.
In the echoes of giggles, we find our way,
Together forever, come what may!

Enchanted Steps

With a hop and a skip, we start our day,
In a whirlwind of fun, we dance and play.
Our feet can't keep quiet, oh what a spree,
In this comical ballet, just you and me.

We twinkle like stars in a confetti night,
With our jumbled moves, everything feels right.
A sideways shimmy, a fumble turned grace,
In this merry mash-up, we find our place.

With pants that are sparkly, shirts mismatched,
Every silly blunder passionately hatched.
As we shimmy past fences and weave through the trees,
In our quirky little realm, we dance as we please.

So let's sway and sway till we're dizzy and keen,
In this tangle of joy, we're simply a dream.
With laughter in pockets and smiles all around,
In our enchanted steps, pure bliss is found.

The Tango of Tomorrow

When we step on each other's toes,
It's a comedy show, as everyone knows.
Twisting and turning with laughter so bright,
Two left feet never felt so right.

With your wild spins, I start to trip,
We laugh as we fumble, just let it slip.
A two-step mishap, we embrace the fall,
In this dance of life, we're having a ball.

Whirling like windmills in a gusty breeze,
Who knew the rhythm would come with such ease?
In mismatched shoes, we take our chance,
Life's a tango that makes us dance.

Tomorrow's steps are yet to emerge,
With your clumsy moves, I feel the urge.
So lead the way, with a grin and a joke,
In our tango of laughs, we never choke.

Pirouettes and Pathways

On this path built from giggles and grins,
You spin like a top, where laughter begins.
With every slick turn, you create a mess,
As I try to keep up, I can't help but guess.

Our feet may stumble, our hearts are in sync,
In a waltz of witticisms, we wink and we blink.
With pirouettes that make the world spin fast,
We laugh at the echoes of our silly past.

Side-stepping puddles and dodging the rain,
Each puddle a stage for our goofy refrain.
The pathways of pranks create silly sights,
As we twirl and we whirl through our zany flights.

So take my hand in this twisty affair,
A bottle of laughter, nothing can compare.
In our dance of folly, we'll always win,
With pirouettes and pathways, let the fun begin.

Love's Melodic Motion

In the symphony of giggles, we sway with delight,
A few awkward notes, but everything's right.
With your quirky moves and my clumsy flow,
We compose a tune that only we know.

Harmonizing laughter like a joyful refrain,
In this jubilant jam, there's never a pain.
So let's spin around like we've lost track of time,
Our lives a silly rhythm, like jingle and chime.

Your steps like a squirrel, are fast and confused,
As we jiggle and giggle, there's nothing to lose.
In the cadence of chaos, love finds its beat,
You're the melody that makes me feel complete.

So here's to the music, let's give it a whirl,
In our dance of laughs, who needs a pearl?
With notes that tickle, and beats that we share,
In the melody of love, we float through the air.

Footprints on Stardust

With each step we take on this cosmic floor,
There's glitter and laughter, who could ask for more?
Our footprints on stardust make quite a scene,
As we trip over joy, it's pure and serene.

We leap through the galaxies, hand in hand,
My tall tales of tripping, they always expand.
With smiles like comets, we illuminate the night,
Our love's a rocket with silly delight.

In the interstellar dance, the twirls never end,
You're the cosmic partner, my bestest friend.
With wigs of confetti and shoes made of light,
We glide through the universe, what a wild sight!

So let's twirl and whirl 'neath the starry embrace,
With laughter as stardust, we find our own space.
In this whimsical journey of playful cheer,
Your hand in mine, there's nothing to fear.

Weaving Through the Tapestry of Time

In a world of colors bright,
We twirl and spin, oh what a sight!
With mismatched socks and silly hats,
We glide around like playful cats.

Through every stitch, we laugh and weave,
Creating memories, we won't believe.
Pinch of chaos, sprinkle of cheer,
In this tapestry, we have no fear.

As clocks tick-tock and winds may gust,
We bounce along, in bliss we trust.
With every thread, our tales unfold,
In this fabric of fun, we're never old.

So grab your partner, don't be shy,
Let's slide and shimmy, oh my, oh my!
Together we're a vibrant rhyme,
Weaving laughter through the sands of time.

In Sync with the Universe

Stars may twinkle, planets swirl,
Yet here we are in our silly whirl.
With joyful hops and quirky prance,
Who needs to follow, when we can dance?

Galaxies laugh, they join our game,
In this cosmic stage, we stake our claim.
With goofy moves, we steal the show,
Parallel to Mars, but we steal the glow.

Gravity's tug can't hold us down,
We spin and twirl with laughter's crown.
In every orbit, we'll find our beat,
Two cosmic clowns on a celestial street.

So let's cha-cha past the Milky Way,
With giggling stars lighting up our play.
In sync with the universe, wild and free,
Together we shine like a happy spree.

A Dance of Hope and Dreams

In a world where hopes take flight,
We leap and lunge, with all our might.
With dreams in pockets, we twirl around,
Each chuckle echoes, a merry sound.

From kitchen floors to open streets,
Every step's a treasure that life bequeaths.
With flips and flops, we take the chance,
In our rhythm, we laugh and prance.

Though life may lead us on quirky trails,
With silly faces, we combat our fails.
In every stumble, we find our stride,
Hope fuels our laughter, as we glide.

So let's raise a glass to dreams and cheer,
A symphony of fun, we hold dear.
In this dance of joy, let's never part,
With hope as our compass, we'll chart our heart.

Entwined in Movement and Melody

With wiggling toes and flailing arms,
We jig and jive, with all our charms.
The music plays, oh what a tune!
We'll shimmy under the glowing moon.

Side by side in this merry race,
We trip and tumble, but find our place.
With laughter as our guide, we flit,
In every little misstep, we won't quit.

As melodies swirl around the air,
Our hearts beat loud without a care.
In every note, our spirits rise,
Two silly birds, we claim the skies.

So pirouette and spin, oh what fun,
Under the sun, we'll never be done.
Entwined in giggles and joy so sweet,
Together we make life's soundtrack complete.

Ties That Bind in Melodic Steps

When you trip and I do a flip,
We laugh like the world is a circus trip.
With mismatched socks and shoes untied,
We groove to the rhythm, side by side.

Our feet might fumble and stumble around,
But in this sweet chaos, joy is found.
You spin like a top, I wobble and sway,
In this silly dance, we'll never stray.

So twirl in the kitchen, let the cat flee,
Slide on the carpet, just you and me.
Each silly move is a joyous sign,
In our grand ballet, we perfectly align.

With a hop and a skip, we take our chance,
Making memories in our clumsy dance.
Who needs a stage when we've got the floor?
In this merry jig, who could ask for more?

Floating on a Sea of Harmony

We float like leaves on a breezy day,
With giggles and wiggles, we sway and play.
Your elbow's a rudder, my knee's a fan,
On this whimsical boat, you're both my friend and tan.

The dog joins in with a bark and a wiggle,
Our symphony's odd, but we dance without giggle.
With splashes of laughter, we sail and glide,
Navigating nonsense, with you by my side.

Our rhythm is off, but who needs a plan?
You lead with a boogie, I follow the span.
Together we drift, on waves of delight,
In our ship of chuckles, everything's right.

As the sun dips low and stars start to gleam,
We float on this ocean, like a silly dream.
With every wide smile, we ride the tide,
In this sea of mirth, forever we'll slide.

Steps Taken with Strength and Grace

With a case of the giggles, you've got two left feet,
But your heart beats wild to this comical beat.
You jump and you spin with a flourish or two,
And I can't help laughing, oh, how you flew!

Around the dining room, we waltz in a trance,
It's a wobbly mess, but oh, what a dance!
You take a bold leap, I catch you just right,
In our zany ballet, we soar through the night.

With arms all a-flapping, and laughter so bright,
We tango through trouble, we pirouette light.
Each step is a story, each twirl is a cheer,
With you as my partner, I'll never fear.

So let's take the plunge into moves so absurd,
Our choreography's crazy, not meant to be heard.
With strength and with grace, we tackle the floor,
In this fun little dance, we're forever more.

The Swing of Moments Shared

In the park with a swing, we take our turns,
With laughter and squeals, the heart gently burns.
You fly through the air like a bird on a quest,
And I'm right behind you, in a chuckling fest.

With a push and a pull, we're lost in the breeze,
Not a care in the world, just you and me, please.
We flip-flop our voices like silly old frogs,
Making tunes in the air, in circles like dogs.

When the sun starts to set, and the shadows grow long,
We sway to the breeze, as we sing our sweet song.
With ropes and with straps, we swing close and tight,
Each moment a treasure, our laughter ignites.

So here's to the swings, to the heights of our bliss,
With giggles and wiggles, we seal our sweet kiss.
As the stars light the sky, our friendship will soar,
In the swing of the night, we'll forever explore.

Hand in Hand on the Path

We tripped on our shoelaces, oh what a sight,
With giggles and grins, we took off in flight.
Two left feet clumsily taking their chance,
In the chaos, we found our own silly dance.

Careening through puddles, we splash and we squeal,
With ice cream on noses, it's quite the appeal.
Sing off-key in the rain, my partner in crime,
Each misstep we take, a new reason to rhyme.

The world spins around us, but we hold it tight,
With one squeeze of the hand, we're ready to fight.
Two jokers on a journey, no maps to confine,
In this circus of life, you're my favorite swine.

As we strut down this path, we giggle and sway,
In this silly parade, we'll dance away gray.
With love and with laughter, let's twirl all we can,
For each twist on our way, we'll make it a plan.

Motion in the Moment

We whirl in our living room, socks on the floor,
Each misstep ends with laughter, I find my way more.
The cat gives a hiss, as we try our best,
To avoid flying coffee, which just adds to the jest.

With cereal for breakfast, we take a big leap,
A pirouette spills milk, oh what a heap!
Your fork becomes a microphone in our hands,
As we belt out the chorus of our favorite bands.

In the middle of chaos, we make our own rules,
Like nimble ballerinas who act like great fools.
Life's like a fast tune, we shimmy and shake,
In this waltz of the wild, we make no mistake.

So here's to the giggles, the silly charades,
In this comedic tango, our worry evades.
Every spin and each twirl is a moment we seize,
With humor as fuel, we glide with such ease.

Together We Flourish

In the garden of chaos, we blossom and grow,
With our tangled up dreams, we put on a show.
Sprouting wild daisies, we dance with the bees,
With pollen on our noses, we're just as we please.

We'll plant all our hopes in this technicolor plot,
With laughter like sunshine, we're quite the hot shot.
Two seedlings entwined in a field of delight,
We tickle each other, then take off in flight.

As weeds try to creep, we just laugh and giggle,
With every odd twist, we shimmy and wiggle.
So if storms tend to gather, let raindrops be fun,
We'll splash in our puddles until we are done.

Together we're sprouted, with roots that entwine,
In the garden of life, you're my favorite vine.
With each bloom that comes forth, we hop and we cheer,
For in this wild dance, it's you I hold dear.

The Pulse of Partnership

With your hand in my pocket, we stroll without care,
Your chuckles and quirks fill the cool evening air.
While clocks tick and tock, we're off on a spree,
In this raucous display, it's just you and me.

We slip on banana peels, laughing so hard,
While dodging the neighbors who think we're quite scarred.
The beat of our footsteps, a silly parade,
In this rhythmic chaos, we've got it made.

With you as my partner, the world's on fast-forward,
We leap over hurdles, our spirits restored.
Two goofballs in sync, we groove to the beat,
With each twist and each turn, life's dance is a treat.

So here's to the laughter, the blunders we find,
In this pulse of our lives, we leave worries behind.
With a wink and a nod, we embrace the bizarre,
For with you by my side, my love, we're a star.

Embrace of the Seasons

In spring we twirl with flowers in bloom,
Our socks mismatched, we spread some gloom.
With winter's chill, we waltz in snow,
Tripping on ice, oh how we glow!

Summer's sun brings hats too wide,
We dance like ducks, and slip and slide.
In autumn's breeze, we leap through leaves,
Or trip on pumpkins, what fun it weaves!

The seasons change, our moves rewind,
We're lost in laughter, silliness defined.
Through sunshine, rain, and snowflakes tight,
We frolic, giggle, what a sight!

With every step, hear the giggled cheers,
As we shuffle through our silly years.
A comical waltz, an embrace divine,
With you by my side, everything's fine!

A Duet of Dreams

In pajamas bright, we sing out loud,
With mismatched socks, we're a silly crowd.
Twirling around with spoons as our mic,
We belt out tunes, oh what a hike!

On a trampoline, we bounce and flip,
Sailing through dreams on a wobbly ship.
With clouds as pillows, we float up high,
Catching the stars as they zoom by!

We dance on cupcakes, frosting on feet,
Every sweet step feels like a treat.
In a whimsical world, where we both belong,
Life's a duet, sweet and strong!

Together we chuckle, through thick and thin,
With each little laugh, our hearts begin.
In this playful dance, there's love and cheer,
As we move through dreams, I'm glad you're here!

Movements of Memory

In our childhood backyard, we chased the sun,
With twirls and tumbles, oh, wasn't it fun?
Swinging so high, we touched the sky,
With a goofy grin, time flashed by!

Through teenage years, we'd strut and pose,
Practicing moves in silly clothes.
Under the disco ball, we'd spin around,
Falling in laughter on the ground!

Our crazy dance-off, where we compete,
With wild moves and no sense of beat.
Each stumble echoes a joyful cheer,
Making memories, oh, how we steer!

Now as we giggle, with gray in our hair,
We still dance whimsically, without a care.
Remembering moments that make us chuckle,
In the book of life, each page is a buckle!

Intertwined Beats

With a clumsy shuffle, we start the show,
Two left feet, but look at us go!
In a skirt made of curtains, we twine and spin,
Giggling loudly as we let the fun in!

With spoons for tambourines, we hammer away,
Creating our symphony, come what may.
A hiccup of laughter, a stumble on cue,
This wild rhythm, just me and you!

In the kitchen, we mix up a brew,
Dancing with flour, and knocking a shoe.
Our culinary waltz, with spices and zest,
You're my partner, you're simply the best!

Amid silly steps and a few slapstick falls,
We sway through the moments, answering calls.
In this merry jig, together we glide,
Intertwined beats, with joy as our guide!